Squirrels

Christine Butterworth

Silver Burdett Press, Morristown, New Jersey

Who do you think likes
to eat nuts?
Who do you think has made
this pile of pinecones?

This red squirrel lives
in this pine tree.
She picks off the pinecones
at the top of the tree.

The squirrel bites off
a pinecone from the tree.
She likes to eat the seeds that
are in the pinecone.

When the squirrel wants
to go to another tree,
she jumps straight across to it.
She does not fall.
Her big tail helps her
to jump and land safely.

Now the squirrel wants to
go down to the ground.
She goes down the tree head-first.
Look at her sharp claws.
These claws help her hold on to the tree.

The squirrel takes a nut to
a tree stump.
See how she uses her front paws
just like hands.

When the squirrel eats a pinecone,
she bites the scales off
with her sharp front teeth.
Now she can get at the seeds.

The squirrel likes to chew
hard nuts and pinecones.
Her front teeth grow all the time.
She chews these hard things into
small pieces to keep her teeth
from growing too long.

These squirrels have found some acorns.
They do not want to eat all
the acorns now.
The squirrels will hide some
of the acorns in secret places.
One squirrel likes to hide her acorns
in an oak tree.

10

This squirrel digs a hole
for her acorns.
She will come back to find
the acorns in the winter.
She will sniff for them.
Then she will dig up
the acorns and eat them.

It is not safe for the squirrel to stay
on the ground too long.
Her red coat is easy to see
in the grass.

A red squirrel is not
big or strong.
She is only as big as a rat,
but her nose can smell danger.
Her ears can hear tiny sounds.

The squirrel watches for danger.

This hawk is hungry.

It wants to find a small animal to eat.

The squirrel sees the hawk.
She runs up the tree quickly
to her nest.
She has made her nest in
a round hole in this hollow tree.
She slips inside the nest.
She stays still and quiet.

The hawk goes away.

The squirrel can come out of her nest.

She finds some berries.

Squirrels like berries

as much as nuts.

Red squirrels live in
pine trees and fir trees.
Gray squirrels do not like these trees.
They like tall trees and
open spaces.
This squirrel lives in an oak tree.

Is there a park or some woods near you?
Are there some tall trees there?
Some gray squirrels may live
near your house.

Gray squirrels like to live
in oak trees and beech trees.
They make their homes in
the branches of these trees.

A gray squirrel makes a flat nest.
It finds some twigs and sticks.
It makes its nest in the fork of a tree.
A gray squirrel has made a nest
in this oak tree.

These two gray squirrels are
chasing each other up the tree.
They are flicking their tails and calling.
Chuck! Chuck!

It is spring.

The two squirrels mate.

In five weeks the female
will have her babies.

22

The female squirrel looks for
a safe place to have her babies.
She finds a hollow tree.
She makes a nest in the hole.
She lines this nest with
dry grass and bits of her own fur.

When the babies are born,
they cannot see.
They cannot hear.
They have no fur.
They have no teeth.

After a week they have some fur.
But they still cannot see.
Their eyes are still closed.

Now they are four weeks old.
Their eyes are open.
They still drink milk
from their mother.

It is summer now.

The babies are seven weeks old.

They have some teeth.

The mother squirrel finds them
food to eat.

The mother squirrel takes
a baby out of the nest.
She picks it up with her teeth.
The baby holds on to the mother.
It curls its long tail around her.

The mother squirrel goes
to find her own food.
She is very hungry.

It is late in the summer now.

The young squirrels leave the nest.

They must watch for
foxes and dogs.

30

Gray squirrels love peanuts.
Children come to this park
to feed the squirrels.
Watch out! Remember that
squirrels have sharp teeth.

The young squirrels make new nests.
Some of them will die
if the winter is very cold.
The others will have families
of their own in the spring.

32

Reading consultant: Diana Bentley
Editorial consultant: Donna Bailey

Illustrated by Paula Chasty
Picture research by Suzanne Williams
Designed by Richard Garratt Design

First published in 1988 by
Macmillan Children's Books,
a division of Macmillan Publishers Limited
4 Little Essex Street, London WC2R 3LF and Basingstoke

Published in the United States by
Silver Burdett Press, Morristown, New Jersey.

Printed in Hong Kong

Library of Congress Cataloging-in-Publication Data
Butterworth, Christine.
    Squirrels.
    (My world)
    Summary: Portrays the habits, behavior, and
characteristics of different kinds of squirrels.
    1. Squirrels——Juvenile literature.   2. Gray
squirrel——Juvenile literature.   3. Tamiasciurus
hudsonicus——Juvenile literature. [1. Squirrels]
I. Chasty, Paula, ill.   II. Title.   III. Series:
Butterworth, Christine.   My world.
QL737.R68B87   1988   599.32'32   87-23399
ISBN 0-382-09556-1

Photographs
Cover: Bruce Coleman/Jane Burton
Bruce Coleman: titlepage (Hans Reinhard), 2 (Jeff Foott), 3, 4, 5
    and 6 (all Hans Reinhard), 7 (Leonard Lee Rue), 9 and 14
    (Hans Reinhard), 15 and 21 (Leonard Lee Rue), 24 (Wayne
    Lankinen)
Eric and David Hosking: 31
Frank Lane Picture Agency: 26 (S. Maslowski), 30 (L. West), 32
    (Mr & Mrs R. P. Lawrence)
NHPA: 11 (S. J. Krasmere)
OSF Picture Library: 16 (D. J. Saunders), 17 and 20 (John
    Paling), 23 and 27 (G. I. Bernard)
Survival Anglia: 25 (Liz and Tony Bomford)
Zefa: 22